BE ANXIOUS FOR NOTHING:

D1360325

BUT PRAY ABOUT EVERYTHING!

Susan J Perry

Copyright Page

Simply This Publishing

Kindle Direct Publishing

*"GOD said it,
I didn't,
GOD told me to tell you!"*

~ Susan J. Perry ~

Deuteronomy 32:3-4

Because I will publish the name of the LORD: ascribe ye greatness unto our God. He is the Rock, his work is perfect: for all his ways are judgment: a God of truth and without iniquity, just and right is he.

CHAPTERS INDEX

CENTRAL TRUTH

GOD is our only hope and there is no other. Don't worry, be happy! If we are rooted and grounded in Him we will not stumble or fall or be carried away by any strange wind of doctrine. But stay firm in our foundation of hope, growing exponentially in Christ Jesus our Lord, maturing and prospering all along the way. You will not be moved by the storms of life that come and go but stand firm in the truth that is within us. Fear has no reason to come in as we stay filled with the Word. This book is based on these scriptures:

Philippians 4:6-7
6 Be anxious for nothing, but in everything by prayer and supplication, with thanksgiving, let your requests be made known to God;

7 and the peace of God, which surpasses all understanding, will guard your hearts and minds through Christ Jesus.

DEDICATION

Our dedication must always truly be to the One true-living God Almighty. It is only He that can save us from this malady of mistrust and misguided emotions we are plagued with day to day, now as we lean in on Him here to get to the truth of the matter.

Thank You Lord for all that you will give us in these tenuous situations because people's emotions need to be healed and delivered by the crowning glory of God. As we get into your presence Lord we can see clearly the fix that we need is in Jesus Christ our Lord and the Holy Ghost in power as they take us boldly into the Throne of Grace and humbly bow down to your sovereignty and majesty. We are in need of you today as you take us into the Glory-Zone of your love and care, we submit ourselves to you in a new way. Help us oh Lord to walk free before you.

Thank You Lord for all those who will be touched by this book; inspired by this book and carried over to victory by this book as the Word is spoken on each page of this book each day just for you. Now devote yourself to God's purposes today. We praise your name!

Psalm 150:6
Let every thing that hath breath praise the LORD. Praise ye the LORD.

INTRODUCTION

Anxiety is another weapon formed against you from the enemy! Do you honestly believe you should receive it? We reject those things by faith and God gave you and I authority over everyone created off-handedly by the enemy. The scriptures say it will NOT prosper!

Isaiah 54:17
"No weapon formed against you shall prosper, And every tongue which rises against you in judgment You shall condemn. This is the heritage of the servants of the LORD, And their righteousness is from Me," Says the LORD.

When will we as God's people truly believe ALL of the Word of God? When will we stand on ALL of His promises? Isaiah 54:17 speaks truth for all of us. Let's break it down:

1. No weapon formed against you shall prosper
2. Everything spoken against you shall be condemned
3. This is our heritage as servants of the Lord
4. And the righteousness of the Lord comes from Him and is our portion as children of God

The Lord in this scripture is speaking promises to His servants, His people. We have this inheritance as children of God and we have authority over everything evil trying to torment us while serving Almighty God. Your blessed assurance is Jesus Christ, so as we trust this information, then our worries and inconsistencies must stop. The Bible states it as so, as Jesus empowered His disciples, then so are we empowered today as His followers:

Luke 9:1
Then he called his twelve disciples together, and gave them power and authority over all devils, and to cure diseases

AND

Luke 10:19
Behold, I give unto you power to tread on serpents and scorpions, and over all the power of the enemy: and nothing shall by any means hurt you.

We have the power to battle anxiety all day long if we must as believers in Jesus Christ. We should be anxious for nothing because we trust God; because the Word says so and it is truth. Why don't we believe it? This is the operable question: Do we trust God? What must we fear, no absolutely nothing as scripture says over and over again! Let us heed scripture and believe it as truth.

Let's get into this book and see what the Holy Spirit will give us on this matter as we meditate on the Word of God and its precepts of truth. Hope and care is like a beautiful bouquet of spring flowers. Let's begin to declare God's Word aloud today and see the change that is coming for you, like a fresh breath of these spring flowers pictured, as their beautiful aroma enters your nostrils each new day, be refreshed!

Give up stress and worry, anxiety and strife because God has given you life and life more abundantly. (John 10:10) God assures us freedom from all bondage!

Special Thanks...

To Elsie Counterman... A woman of inspiration and Godly love towards many! A flautist, a poet, a prayer warrior and a spirit-filled woman of God who will pray for you at the drop of a hat! It's you we wrote this book for certainly. You have inspired us, I hope you enjoy it and it helps many. Thank you very much for all your special ways!

Isaiah 54:17
No weapon that is formed against thee shall prosper; and every tongue that shall rise against thee in judgment thou shalt condemn. This is the heritage of the servants of

the LORD, and their righteousness is of me, saith the LORD.

Amen.

Frank & Karen Sumrall... Thank you for all your parental care and spiritual love over the years; your guidance has been more valuable than rubies and we love you very much! As we go through the fires of life together, we recognize you as family and our bond is great as the Lord takes us to higher heights and deeper depths, we are being prepared for each stage that the Lord sets for us. Again, thank you very much! It has been one of those sweet pleasures that God gives us.

Proverbs 7:4 (TLB)
Love wisdom like a sweetheart; make her a beloved member of your family.

John Perry... Love you John Perry, my husband. You have been a good one especially now as our publisher, we have come a long way together.

We are Team Jesus as I had vowed many years ago in prayer. Some look at us crazy like we are some weird phenomena but we know who we are as God inspires us to do more. Seeking Him together in prayer has brought forth so many big results. Thanks again for your love and devotion to God, family and me.

Isaiah 22:23-24 (TLB)
"I will make of him a strong and steady peg to support my people; they will load him with responsibility, and he will be an honor to his family name."

OUR PRAYER... Is that no one will remain the same after reading and studying this book, but deliverance will take place easily through scriptures and prayers as good results before God's Throne of Grace. Come and partake in this special love of God and mercy for all mankind to be rid of anxiety and stress once and for all:

GO NOW IN JESUS MIGHTY NAME>>>>>>>AMEN!

CHAPTER ONE

The Crux of Anxiety

This book is to help those who have succumbed to this layer of fear called anxiety and we must get to the crux of this thing to help others. As in the title of this book, the Bible says to be anxious for nothing in the NKJV of Philippians 4:6-7. Different versions call anxiety different things. I am going to quote you different versions here to see how they unmask this malady so much more expertly. Let's take a look:

1. Philippians 4:6-7
King James Version

*6 **Be careful for nothing**; but in every thing by prayer and supplication with thanksgiving let your requests be made known unto God.*

7 And the peace of God, which passeth all understanding, shall keep your hearts and minds through Christ Jesus.

2. Philippians 4:6-7
Living Bible

*6 **Don't worry about anything**; instead, pray about everything; tell God your needs, and don't forget to thank him for his answers.*

7 If you do this, you will experience God's peace, which is far more wonderful than the human mind can understand. His peace will keep your thoughts and your hearts quiet and at rest as you trust in Christ Jesus.

3. Philippians 4:6-7
The Message

*6 **Don't fret or worry**. Instead of worrying, pray. Let petitions and praises shape your worries into prayers, letting God know your concerns.*

7 Before you know it, a sense of God's wholeness, everything coming together for good, will come and settle you down. It's wonderful what happens when Christ displaces worry at the center of your life

4. Philippians 4:6-7
Amplified Bible

*6 **Do not be anxious or worried about anything**, but in everything [every circumstance and situation] by prayer and petition with thanksgiving, continue to make your [specific] requests known to God.*

7 And the peace of God [that peace which reassures the heart, that peace] which transcends all understanding, [that peace which] stands guard over your hearts and your minds in Christ Jesus [is yours].

5. Philippians 4:6-7
Contemporary English Version

*6 **Don't worry about anything**, but pray about everything. With thankful hearts offer up your prayers and requests to God.*

7 Then, because you belong to Christ Jesus, God will bless you with peace that no one can completely understand. And this peace will control the way you think and feel.

6. Philippians 4:6-7
New International Version

*6 **Do not be anxious about anything**, but in every situation, by prayer and petition, with thanksgiving, present your requests to God.*

7 And the peace of God, which transcends all understanding, will guard your hearts and your minds in Christ Jesus.

7. Philippians 4:6-7
New King James Version

6 ***Be anxious for nothing**, but in everything by prayer and supplication, with thanksgiving, let your requests be made known to God;*

7 and the peace of God, which surpasses all understanding, will guard your hearts and minds through Christ Jesus.

I have given you seven different translation versions of this scripture to give it complete clarity in every way possible. But as we may notice the first words in each scripture typed which I have bolded in the sentences many are in accord with each other as they descriptively say, ***"Do not!"***

The different versions call this malady: care, fret, worry and anxiety (anxious); all negative emotions that must be dealt with because they are ungodly and warned against in this text. Let's get a definition of anxiety and see what it says. In my spirit the word 'trepidation' is coming through loud and clear and fear is at the root of this.

Anxiety
noun

anx·i·ety | \ aŋ-ˈzī-ə-tē \
plural **anxieties**

Essential Meaning of *anxiety*

1: fear or nervousness about what might happen; feelings of anger and *anxiety*. She suffers from chronic/acute *anxiety*.

2: a feeling of wanting *to do* something very much. She has always had an *anxiety to succeed*. [=she has always been anxious to succeed]

Full Definition of anxiety

(1): apprehensive uneasiness or nervousness usually over an impending or anticipated ill: a state of being
 (2) *medical:* an abnormal and overwhelming sense of apprehension and fear often marked by physical signs (such as tension, sweating, and increased pulse rate), by doubt concerning the reality and nature of the threat, and by self-doubt about one's capacity to cope with it
b: mentally distressing concern or interest
c: a strong desire sometimes mixed with doubt, fear, or uneasiness... Ex: his *anxiety* to succeed and his continued nervousness over the possible bankruptcy of his shoe company caused her to lecture him about relaxing and caring for his health.
2: a cause of anxiety... citizens stressed by gnawing economic and social *anxieties.*

Synonyms for anxiety

- agita,
- agitation,
- anxiousness,
- apprehension,
- apprehensiveness,
- care,
- concern,
- concernment,
- disquiet,
- disquietude,
- fear,
- nervosity,
- nervousness,
- perturbation,
- solicitude,
- sweat,
- unease,
- uneasiness,
- worry

Antonyms

- unconcern

Apparently by these definitions, synonyms and antonyms, anxiety is way too much concern for oneself. When we are into anxiety and or fear we are into self and the center of that self. It is an inward projection causing an outward manifestation of fear-based anxiety often causing sickness and weakness of the spirit within.

This anxiety and fear paralyzes one so they will not have to perform what is expected of them. Their commitment to fear is greater than their commitment to the truth. They are overwhelmed by this malady unable to move or perform a task. Their mode of operation gets shut down unfortunately, and this is what the enemy employs them to do by the spirit of fear and the impossibilities of anxiety to grip their very nature and withhold their good God-given gifts.

The crux of this thing is that anxiety has become a medical disorder in the world which medicates everything and psychoanalyzes everything and we can see many people suffer with this in today's world. But the Body of Christ must know better and learn to trust in the Lord implicitly with everything, we cast our cares upon Him and accept the peace of God, only He offers. How do we get this? Well, we get it in salvation although many veer away and even walk away; fear overtakes the little they had of God. We must then rededicate our lives to the Lord knowing He reigns over all that we live for and even that which torments us; there is victory to be had.

This is apparently a subject that the Lord wishes to deal with in His Body because He told me to write a book about it, in line with many others; anxiety is a real well-known concern and needs to be dealt with. If you know and love Jesus, then you should NOT be experiencing anxiety or fear. It is not of God. It is of satan himself and regularly adding a tormenting spirit with it.

2 Timothy 1:7
For God has not given us
a spirit of fear, but of power
and of love and of a sound mind.

Anxiety and fear as you can see by this scripture does not originate with God, but it is a mental issue which plagues the mind of man, a tormenting of sorts by evil forces. It often originates with the intimidation of these spirits as one feels inadequate to do the job God has given. Moses speaks of this because he stuttered yet God sent him to Pharaoh to free the Israelites.

Exodus 4:10
And Moses said unto the LORD, O my LORD, I am not eloquent, neither heretofore, nor since thou hast spoken unto thy servant: but I am slow of speech, and of a slow tongue.

In this operation to free the slaves of Israel from Egypt, God sent Aaron with Moses to go as a team to speak to Pharaoh and get the job done.

Sometimes we cannot do it alone but must employ teamwork because the job God calls us to do is so much bigger than one man can handle singly. (Or so we think) Or as a confidence builder which God always is, we are encouraged with this help to build. The Bible says two is better than one in Ecclesiastes 4:9.

In the next chapter we will talk about the symptoms of anxiety and negativity which are formulated in man from fear. Many books are written about the battlefield of the mind or the entry way for demonic activity. We must as followers of Christ, tend our gates and be careful of our surroundings.

PLEASE DECLARE WITH US TODAY: "We declare we are anxious for nothing but pray about everything, in Jesus mighty name, amen!"

CHAPTER TWO

The Symptoms of Anxiety

Fear and anxiety go hand-in-hand with one another as they cause misery in a person's life and yes believer's as well; as the world deals with this, and some on a daily basis even. It's a word one might call as, *"psychotic."* This has come into my spirit so let's define this word as well to get a clearer view of it:

Psychotic
adjective

psy·chot·ic | \ sī-ˈkä-tik \

1 *medical*: of, relating to, marked by, or affected with psychosisa, *psychotic* patient, *psychotic* behavior

2 *sometimes offensive:* exhibiting or suggestive of mental or emotional unsoundness or instability —not used technically

NOTE: The non-technical use of psychotic is increasingly viewed as a trivialization of mental illness.

Symptoms of Anxiety Disorder:

Panic, fear, uneasiness; feelings of panic or doom, or danger or sleep problems; not being able to stay calm and still (at peace); cold, sweaty, numb, or tingling hands or feet, shortness of breath; hyperventilation; heart palpitations; dry mouth; nausea; tense muscles; dizziness; thinking about a problem over and over again and unable to stop (rumination;) inability to concentrate; intensely or obsessively avoiding feared objects or places.

Panic Attacks:

Panic attacks are sudden periods of intense fear that comes on one quickly and reach their peak intensity in a few minutes. This is triggered by a fear of a certain object or situation. Symptoms experienced during these attacks: heart palpitations; sweating, trembling, or shaking sensations or shortness of breath, smothering or choking; feelings of impending doom, feelings of being out of control.

Let me please say something first here after researching all these related symptoms I have come to one major conclusion:

WE ALL NEED JESUS!

The Bible says this:

1 Peter 5:6-7
6 Therefore humble yourselves
under the mighty hand of God, that
He may exalt you in due time,

7 casting all your care upon Him,
for He cares for you.

All these symptoms listed here
must go in Jesus name. He is your
help in the time of need and He is
your Redeemer and Savior and the
solution for everything you desire or
need. Symptoms are lies of the
enemy. The Bible says that the devil
is the father of all lies. So why do we
believe him and mistrust God's
ability to save us from these lies? The
Bible says this:

John 8:44
You are of your father the devil, and
the desires of your father you want
to do. He was a murderer from the
beginning, and does not stand in the
truth, because there is no truth in
him. When he speaks a lie, he speaks
from his own resources, for he is a
liar and the father of it.

You cannot believe one word this monster says about you or anyone else. Don't let him torment you any longer but cast all your cares upon Jesus who is the giver of life and not the prognosticator of death as satan is. We have no part of his world which is full of lies and deception.

There is nothing the devil has to offer us that is worth our salvation or our close walk with the Lord. When this attack tries to come upon your life, remember Adam and Eve when sin came into the garden that fateful day. They lost everything! Sure, they still had their lives but God cursed them because of their sin and became separated from God. Today the ripple effect of that original sin still plays a part in this ole world today, some thousands of years later.

We must repent and turn away from these things if we hope for a deeper walk with the Lord. Do not let fear or anxiety impede your progress on your life's journey but cast it off and get delivered today!

I remember having panic attacks before I knew Jesus and it felt like a heart attack. Your panic is attacking you inwardly because it too is rooted in fear. Panic is a frightening exercise which usually has fruitless results. Nothing good can come out of panic except maybe a helping hand or a big hug from another. Doctors cannot cure it but only medicate it and put you in a stupor by prescription to rest. You will close your eyes to the outside world of reality. But only Jesus can deliver you from it if you trust Him enough. Ask Him to take it from you today in prayer. Surely He will.

Fear and anxiety attack you and Jesus needs to deliver you IF: if you know Him; if you love Him and if you obey Him, only then will HE deliver you from the mess you are in. Cry out loud as the blind man did in Mark 10:

Mark 10:47-48
47 And when he heard that it was Jesus of Nazareth, he

began to cry out, and say, Jesus, thou son of David, have mercy on me.

48 And many charged him that he should hold his peace: but he cried the more a great deal, Thou son of David, have mercy on me.

Let's cry out to the Lord today to heal and deliver you and me in Jesus mighty name! No more *psychosis* in Jesus name!

Let's pray:

Dear Jesus,
We need your help! Please take these tormenting spirits away from me named anxiety and fear! Close all these doors and deliver everything from me that is not of YOU! I cast my cares upon you today dear Jesus! Please give me your peace again to soothe every nerve on edge and keep me in good stead with You.

Drive this thing out as far as the east is from the west. I trust in You. In Jesus name we pray. Amen.

CHAPTER THREE

Apply the Blood

1 John 1:7
But if we walk in the light as He is
in the light, we have fellowship with
one another, and the blood of Jesus
Christ His Son cleanses us from
all sin.

The blood of Jesus, nothing but the
blood which washes white as snow;
we sing about it; we preach and
teach about it but do we really know
the power in the blood? Jesus died,
shed His blood and rose again unto
Heaven and the power in His blood
was left behind for us. We can apply
it anytime. In fact when we were

saved to Jesus, the blood was applied to our lives so that when the Father looks down upon us, He only sees the Blood of Jesus. He does not see our imperfections but only the Blood that cleanses us changing us into righteous beings as Jesus was as He walked upon the earth. That's why we keep following Jesus; He is our Shepherd; He is our righteousness. This is our right standing before God Almighty who sits upon the Throne of Heaven who is perfect and holy making us daily more like Him. Take off your shoes, its holy ground before God!

In the Old Testament they used the blood of bulls and birds, lambs and such to kill and put their blood on the holy altars of God to atone for sin. This was their blood covenant at that time. Man cannot live without the blood atonement before a holy God. Be thankful our people received much more grace in a new covenant in the atoning blood shed on Calvary's cross as Jesus died for all mankind and His blood put on the mercy seat of Heaven to keep us safe. God thought of it all. Now we apply the blood by saying it spiritually in prayers and supplications as we declare the power of it to keep us, we and our families.

1 Peter 1:19-21
19 But with the precious blood of Christ, as of a lamb without blemish and without spot:

20 Who verily was foreordained before the foundation of the world, but was manifest in these last times for you,

21 Who by him do believe in God, that raised him up from the dead, and gave him glory; that your faith and hope might be in God.

God's plan was foreordained and we are the blessed ones that walk through this blood covenant unscathed and protected because Jesus remained sinless and perfect as He still is today. Apply the blood and seek the change God has given us and let's keep delivered and set free from anxiety and fear, or any malady the devil tries to give us. We are God's children and we should be unwilling to accept any mess the devil has to offer us. It's never any good! Choose God's plan and not man's as we apply the blood regularly. There is wonder-working power in the blood!

Let's pray:

Dear Jesus,
We come in your holy name,
We ask for forgiveness of sin,
And the lack of trust we must have.
Thank You Lord
For healing and delivering us today,
So we may be free of anxiety and
fear to trust you more.
Close all doors that I have opened
unawares.
In Your name Jesus,
Amen.

CHAPTER FOUR

How is Your Heart?

There always seems to be a heart issue with almost every book we write, so let's examine our hearts today. What is in your heart? Don't let fear, anxiety or stress get into your most important organ. These negative entities will tear it up and leave little behind. This organ retains your life and blood flow and you cannot live without it. You must maintain its urgent care to live as we need to before God. There are many, many scriptures on the heart and that which affects it. Let's start with the two I quote often because they

say so much, both in the Book of
John, chapter 14:

John 14:1
Let not your heart be troubled: ye
believe in God, believe also in me.

AND

John 14:27
Peace I leave with you, my peace I
give unto you: not as the world
giveth, give I unto you. Let not your
heart be troubled, neither let
it be afraid.

John 14:1 talks about trouble in
your heart. What is this trouble in
your heart? Get it out now! Believe in
God and believe on Jesus to deliver
you from this trouble. Then in John
14:27 Jesus states He will give you
His peace. He gives you the solution
to your heart trouble and it is: *Peace.*
Knowing Jesus gives us His peace
which should quell any fear or
anxiety in your heart. Then there
should be no trouble in it. Jesus died
to give us His peace. He sent His

Holy Spirit as He resurrected unto Father and made the Apostles wait 50 days in the Upper Room unto Pentecost. Jesus sent the Comforter. Comfort=Peace. John spoke of the Comforter 4 times in scripture:

1. John 14:16

*And I will pray the Father, and he shall give you another **Comforter**, that he may abide with you for ever;*

2. John 14:26

*But the **Comforter**, which is the Holy Ghost, whom the Father will send in my name, he shall teach you all things, and bring all things to your remembrance, whatsoever I have said unto you.*

3. John 15:26

*But when the **Comforter** is come, whom I will send unto you from the Father, even the Spirit of truth, which proceedeth from the Father, he shall testify of me:*

4. John 16:7

*Nevertheless I tell you the truth; It is expedient for you that I go away: for if I go not away,
the **Comforter** will not come unto you; but if I depart, I will send him unto you.*

Jesus wanted us to be comforted. *"Let not your heart be troubled!"* No, we have the Comforter in the Holy Spirit on the inside of us. Why are we troubled; why are we fretting and worrying needlessly. God gave us the Holy Spirit in salvation and the Fire in baptism of the Holy Spirit and we cannot and must not ignore Him, for He is the Spirit of Wisdom who knows all things. Just seek Him. Read these scriptures; study them and know them so you will be reassured of the comfort God has given you.

Let's define comfort for those who are really troubled:

Com·fort

/ˈkəmfərt/

Noun

- 1.a state of physical ease and freedom from pain or constraint: "room for four people to travel in comfort"

- 2. the easing or alleviation of a person's feelings of grief or distress: "a few words of comfort." Similar: consolation; solace; condolence; sympathy. Opposite of grief.

It is very tempting to let trouble get into our hearts. We feel sorry for ourselves for our situation and blame God at times. Why didn't He help me? The questions come in doubt and fear but my question to you is: Did you ask Him to help you? Did you cry out to Him as we supposed? What brought this on?

Psalm 34:17
The righteous cry, and the LORD heareth, and delivereth them out of all their troubles.

Is that you today? Cry out for help from the Lord and He will answer you. It may not be the way that you think but God knows best and will give you the best as He answers your distress. Turn it over to Him. Do not keep it in your heart. It may destroy your life force otherwise. You need a strong heart! You need the life that flows through this organ!

I remember when I was diagnosed with colon cancer; I had successful surgery and sought God for healing throughout the process. I wasn't distressed but I followed the discernment God has given me, thankfully. And suddenly I heard the Lord's voice speak sweetly in our church service one day, saying, *"Go to Psalm 30:2."* So I did, I got my Bible and turned to my most favorite scripture today; one you could hang onto too. Here it is:

Psalm 30:2
O LORD my God, I cried unto thee, and thou hast healed me.

What a glorious day that was! What a testimony I have to encourage others and I can encourage you now, to trust in God who heals us and sets us free. It is His good pleasure to give you the desires of your heart!

Luke 12:32
Fear not, little flock; for it is your Father's good pleasure to give you the kingdom.

In the Book of Isaiah there is a prophecy which still exists noting the birth of our God as He is named:

Isaiah 9:6
For unto us a child is born, unto us a son is given: and the government shall be upon his shoulder: and his name shall be called Wonderful, Counsellor, The mighty God, The everlasting Father, The Prince of Peace.

How can you be troubled now after reading these beautiful names? *"For unto us,"* *This* child was born and given to us, the believers of

Jehovah God, and His name is
"Jesus!"

Get your heart right with Jesus;
through Jesus and in Jesus we can
have good things which do not have
to include trouble. Jesus always
spoke peace to the troubled waters.
He is the Prince of Peace.

There are actually two kinds of
hearts according to the Book of
Ezekiel: A **stony heart** and a **heart
of flesh**.

Ezekiel 36:26
A new heart also will I give you, and
a new spirit will I put within you:
and I will take away
the stony heart out of your flesh,
and I will give you an heart of flesh.

Which heart do you have? I picture
the heart of stone, hard and
calloused because the world has been
hard on that one. It may contain
(besides the world) unforgiveness;
anger; bitterness; envy; jealousy;
lust; greed; lying; chaos; tumult,

covetousness, murder and sin. When all these things are removed from the heart of stone to become the heart of flesh, all is plucked out and forgiven in salvation and washed by the blood of Jesus; cleansed as white as snow; Forgotten by our Father in Heaven.

Your heart should be softened and more flesh-like in texture rather than hard and calloused as before. Blood can flow through it easier and life is extended as we know and love Jesus, our life-giver! He changed everything! Now come on and get rid of that nasty stuff in your heart if you have any of it today. Examine yourselves:

2 Corinthians 13:5
Examine yourselves, whether ye be in the faith; prove your own selves. Know ye not your own selves, how that Jesus Christ is in you, except ye be reprobate

Let's pray:

Dear Jesus,
We love you and come in your holy name;
Bless us oh Lord with a clean heart;
A fresh start and new beginnings as we go forth here.
Thank you Lord for purging any impurities from our hearts,
And forgiving us for anything we were deceived by,
We forgive those who have hurt us.
Remove the veil and let us see.
Grow us up in a greater discernment so we may protect ourselves,
From this ever happening again.
In Jesus name, amen.

CHAPTER FIVE

The Prince of Peace

He is the SAR Shalom of God; the Prince of Peace and the Everlasting Father, the Soon Coming King and the Lover of my soul. He is our Redeemer, our Savior and the Deliverer of any malady we need deliverance from. He is so much bigger!! This takes me back to a thought when we asked our babies, *"How big?"* And they smiled big stretched their arms horizontally out from their sides and shouted, ***"SO BIG!"*** And we all agreed! This is our God. He is far bigger and better than our outstretched arms but His magnitude is not for us to decipher but to gaze in wonderment about when we see Him face to face for the very first time in Heaven and we will be in awe and wonder!

He will clean you up and close all doors to evil which have been inadvertently opened to fear, anxiety or stress but will replace it all with the peace of God that passes all understanding. If you do not know Jesus any other way, please know He is the Prince of Peace. We have talked about this in the previous chapter but let's go deeper here:

John 14:27
Peace I leave with you, My peace I give to you; not as the world gives do I give to you. Let not your heart be troubled, neither let it be afraid.

This scripture is so reassuring made by Jesus notated in the Book of John; the disciple Jesus loved. Jesus keeps stating the obvious until we understand, until we fully give our lives over to Him and surrender ALL. Then you will know His peace and cast out all those negative emotions that you have been dealing with. We must know Him intimately to flow in His peace. In Isaiah of the Old Testament, we get an even deeper picture:

Isaiah 66:12
For thus saith the LORD, Behold, I will extend peace to
her like a river, and the glory of the Gentiles like a flowing stream: then shall ye suck, ye shall be borne upon her sides, and be dandled upon her knees.

Our peace must flow like a river in the glory of our God. It changes our lives completely. I write in the River of God as the Spirit gives me utterance and knowledge that I know nothing about. This book for instance keeps flowing because Father wants it written because He loves His children and wants them ready for the Bridegroom. He desires our hearts right before Him! We must be healed and delivered, cleaned up to prepare for this upcoming wedding we saints are going to. My husband and I are in ministry to do just that according to my understanding and relationship with the Father. He is preparing us for those things to come. We will celebrate altogether!

Our emotions must come under subjection. Its time to hop off that long bumpy ride and get on the ride of your life in the palm of the Father's right hand to bring you to victory over every plan of the enemy, who is already, defeated by Jesus Christ our Lord!

The SAR Shalom of God is Jesus the Prince of Peace! The scripture that goes with this name is:

Psalm 29:11
The LORD will give strength unto his people; the LORD will bless his people with peace.

This scripture is amazing in all that it says our peace is a blessing from God and it gives us strength. We all need strength don't we? We need it each and every day! Our God takes care of His people when He is the SAR Shalom of your life. We must know and love peace. The beatitudes which Jesus preached in the Book of Matthew, chapter 5 says:

Matthew 5:9
Blessed are the peacemakers: for they shall be called the children of God.

This is a cool promise for those of us who know peace because we are called *'the peacemakers'* and *'the children of God.'* This is real relationship. Peace is a real attribute of God and His nature. So should we be.

Keeping your peace in today's times is not always easy. It used to be said that Police Officers were labeled as Peace Officers and they tried to keep the peace in their community, city and state. Today they try to keep trouble off the streets, but it has become very difficult in these times of lawlessness! This is an ugly spirit running around trying to take over! Leadership or a small faction of our country is trying to defund our police and put them out of business! Can you imagine that? Chaos would reign! Everything seems out of order and the days are going by fast as well. We must get a grip and grab a hold of some true peace and quiet, so we can live amicably. How do we live with a nation which is in unrest and deep corruption beyond our reach? We pray and believe God is a just God! He will have the final say and not man! Put down that newspaper and magazine and keep the news far at bay and continue with the peace steady in your home; your heart and your mind as the space around you is peacefully quiet. All unto the glory of God!

Let's pray:

Dear Jesus,
We come in your name;
You are the Holy One,

We seek Your peace
To steady our lives,
And keep us in your good stead.
For every bump we encounter,
We are going to call upon,
The Prince of Peace,
And our Lord and Savior,
In Jesus mighty name we pray,
amen!

CHAPTER SIX

The Light Will Deliver the Darkness

GET OUT OF THE DARKNESS!!

The first thing Father did in creating the universe is speak light into existence. In other words: He turned the lights on for all of us, He welcomed us into His realm. Won't you come into His atmosphere today and seek His wisdom for this tireless malady of any kind, the light will chase it away; it will go back into its own darkness and leave you!

Genesis 1:3-5
3 And God said, Let there be light:
and there was light.

4 And God saw the light, that it was
good: and God divided
the light from the darkness.

5 And God called the light Day, and
the darkness he called Night. And
the evening and the morning were
the first day.

And it was good. Everything the
Lord does is good! We as believers
have no doubt of that, do we? God's
creation began with the light and
although that may sound simple to
you and me because we have taken it
for granted for so long, God
delivered the darkness of the
universe into the light of His nature
because He is the light. What did
Jesus say in scripture?

John 8:12
Then spake Jesus again unto them,
saying, I am the light of the world:
he that followeth me shall not

walk in darkness, but shall
have the light of life.

When we are walking in fear, anxiety and stress, we are heading towards the darkness, exiting God's light. It is not a place where God exists because you must seek Him. Those things are not of our God because He delivered us of those trepidations as we came into the light of His salvation for He is the light. Again, I must say that when you go into a dark room, turn the light switch on, darkness flees immediately. You cannot find one iota of darkness in that room as the light floods in and overtakes it. You can keep looking for a speck of darkness until you turn the light back off, and kick Jesus out of your life. But you won't find it. Please don't ever do that. Do not give in to the darkness, ever, ever. It is a terrible place to be!

I recently wrote a book titled: Lessons In Deliverance, the Lord downloaded the precepts for it when

I started an afternoon nap one day. He showed me first of all *"The Light delivers the darkness,"* and then He gave me the understanding. It was pretty outstanding that day, because I did not think I was capable of writing on deliverance, but God knows about it all and I serve the Master. He inspires and writes the books by the Holy Spirit as He is doing this one too. I know nothing, but He knows it all! He fills me with His light and understanding!

We need the light to live fruitfully. How would anything grow or prosper without the light? We need the light for photosynthesis. How would we be living in total darkness? Nothing would grow or stay alive; depression and evil would be preeminent everywhere. Is that what we want? We must have the light and walk in it with the Lord Jesus Christ, so our lives are full of His light so that others may see. We have His marvelous light within us. How blessed we are!

1 Peter 2:9
But ye are a chosen generation, a royal priesthood, an holy nation, a peculiar people; that ye should shew forth the praises of him who hath called you out of darkness into his marvellous light;

God has been so good to us in everything, just look around and if you see any darkness, cast it out in Jesus mighty name!! You serve a God of Light. Look at the above verse of scripture and read it again and again until you get it engraved upon your heart:

"You are a chosen generation, a royal priesthood, a holy nation, a peculiar people who God called out of the darkness into his marvelous light."

This is such blessing as we will have eternal life with Him forever and ever if we stay in the Light and keep His precepts, it is a surety. Do not turn back to your old ways or your old world but march forward

faithfully in the promises of God
which are for us. He has set you free;
don't go back into bondage and the
slavery of sin. Let nothing come
between you and God, stay in the
light. It's much healthier!

John 12:35
Then Jesus said unto them, Yet a
little while is the light with you.
Walk while ye have the light,
lest darkness come upon you: for he
that walketh in darkness knoweth
not whither he goeth.

AND

Ephesians 5:11
And have no
fellowship with the unfruitful works
of darkness, but rather
reprove them.

AND

1 John 1:6
If we say that we have
fellowship with him, and walk

*in darkness, we lie, and do
not the truth:*

So thankful for the light in our lives because there was a time I could not see or hear because I was deaf and blind in the world without Jesus. Step back, take a look and give thanks today. God has done great things for us: He has turned on the lights for us and paid the electricity bill eternally with the Lord Jesus Christ. Stay close and draw near, darkness will keep trying to come in but don't allow it. It is NOT your portion.

Let's pray:

*Dear Jesus,
We come in your precious name;
We ask you to keep the lights on for us,
Welcome us back home;
So we may never walk in darkness again.
We love your light and are warmed by it.*

Thank You for paying the bill too,
We love you Lord and ask Your help today,
Keep us free to live, love and breathe your precepts
For eternal life!
In Jesus mighty name, amen.

CHAPTER SEVEN

The Hidden Agenda

For me as I see it and as the Holy Spirit points out to me that anxiety is often hidden inward in a person and the outward person is unaware of these hidden devises, plots and plans of an adversary that is so deceptive or clandestined to bring you to failure or in some cases to death ultimately. What does John 10:10 say:

The thief does not come except to steal, and to kill, and to destroy. I have come that they may have life, and that they may have it more abundantly.

Sometimes we as a people are not wily enough to know that he is there trying to trick you; steal from you or even kill you with his lies. We must acknowledge his presence in our lives and kick him out for good! We opened the door of fear through this anxiety we suffer with and he has had legal right to torment you but let's get rid of him now, once and forever! Close the doors to fear; open the doors to faith and apply the blood as we have spoken of in chapters before. The liar cannot cross the blood-line of Jesus Christ, ever!

Hidden agendas hide in the heart of a matter. We look around and see who was fooled by a man-made created pandemic, which killed so many. Mankind has really suffered behind this created folly! So this same man or team of men created a vaccine to kill and maim those who remained. This is a widespread deception by the enemy of our lives. Many succumbed to this tyranny as it continues to run on maliciously today. Only our true and Living God can change things now. America must repent and turn from its wickedness totally. The door has long been opened to unrepentant evil. Abortion and killing young babies is murder and what do the Ten Commandments say?

Exodus 20:13 Thou shalt not kill.

Our God does not change or turn from the law created for His people. Jesus repeated those commandments in the Book of Matthew:

Matthew 19:17-19
17 And he said unto him, Why callest thou me good? there is none good but one, that is, God: but if thou wilt enter into life, keep the commandments.

*18 He saith unto him, Which? Jesus said, **Thou shalt do no murder,** Thou shalt not commit adultery, Thou shalt not steal, Thou shalt not bear false witness,*

19 Honour thy father and thy mother: and, Thou shalt love thy neighbour as thyself.

   If we cannot keep these commandments we are walking in the darkness, definitely, opposing God's will for us. What is your hidden agenda if you have one? Can it be worry, fear, anxiety, stress or worse: sin? It's time to fess up and draw close to God while we repent and turn away from such as these. This is what Saint Peter teaches us in scripture:

1 Peter 3:4
But let it be the hidden man of the heart, in that which is not corruptible, even the ornament of a meek and quiet spirit, which is in the sight of God of great price.

   We must be incorruptible on the inwards parts and keep the Word of God in our hearts. We are ornaments of great price in the sight of God. We look around and know many who have hidden agendas in their hearts that we recognize as sinful but without judgment we bow before the King of Glory and ask to be cleansed of anything hidden. We know God searches the heart. Cry unto the Lord as David did!

Psalm 51:5-11
5 Behold, I was shapen in iniquity; and in sin did my mother conceive me.

6 Behold, thou desirest truth in the inward parts: and in the hidden part thou shalt make me to know wisdom.

7 Purge me with hyssop, and I shall be clean: wash me, and I shall be whiter than snow.

8 Make me to hear joy and gladness; that the bones which thou hast broken may rejoice.

9 Hide thy face from my sins, and blot out all mine iniquities.

10 Create in me a clean heart, O God; and renew a right spirit within me.

11 Cast me not away from thy presence; and take not thy holy spirit from me.

Come and get purified by the Word of God that washes us clean again and again. Please know the agenda of your heart. Meditate on it! If you do not seem to know what is inside your heart then seek God because it is He that searches our hearts. He knows all.

Psalm 139:23
Search me, O God, and know my heart: try me, and know my thoughts:

AND

Romans 8:27
And he who searches our hearts knows the mind of the Spirit, because the Spirit intercedes for

God's people in accordance with the will of God.
Amen.

Let's pray:

Dear Jesus,
Your life for mine;
Your name will cleanse me,
And make me whole again!
Cleanse and purge our hearts,
From all unrighteousness.
We are seeking your blood to cleanse us again,
Dear Lord, our Savior, Redeemer and, Soon Coming King!
In your mighty name Jesus,
Amen.

CHAPTER EIGHT

Disorder: What is it?

1 Corinthians 14:40
Let all things be done decently and in order.

How many know God is a God of order? When He spoke creation into being, it was a process of order. God is still that way, perfect in all His ways.

Deuteronomy 32:4
He is the Rock, His work is perfect;
For all His ways are justice, A God of truth and without injustice;
Righteous and upright is He.

God continues to try and perfect us all along the way here on earth or until we go to be with Him in Heaven. This is being in order.

Paul speaks here in Colossians:

Colossians 2:5
For though I am absent in the flesh, yet I am with you in spirit, rejoicing to see your good order and the steadfastness of your faith in Christ.

Even though Paul is not with us; Jesus is not with us in the flesh of course, we are led in order to the Word of God, our daily guide. Let's define what is disorder:

Definition of disorder (Entry 1 of 2)

transitive verb

1: to disturb the order of
2: to disturb the regular or normal functions of

disorder

noun

Definition *of* disorder (Entry 2 of 2)

1: lack of order: clothes in *disorder*
2: breach of the peace or public order; troubled times marked by social *disorders*
3: an abnormal physical or mental condition; a liver *disorder;* a personality *disorder*

This word disorder goes against the natural order of things or goes against the natural order of God. God set up creation to work in a certain order and when the natural order gets knocked all out of order or off kilter and then we have an imbalance or disorder. What is imbalanced in your life before God? Think on that; pray on that and seek the face of God for relief. There must be balance in our lives because God created it as so. Where did man go wrong? SIN lieth at the door.

Genesis 4:7
If you do well, will you not be
accepted? And if you do not do
well, sin lies at the door. And its
desire is for you, but you should rule
over it."

The Lord warns us early on in the
Book of Genesis (the book of
beginnings) in chapter 4 after the fall
of man. By saying sin lies at the door;
disorder waits for you to mess up.
That will get you all out of the order
God has provided for you as you
misstep your way around the
Kingdom of God.

EX.: Have you ever heard or seen a
wash machine when its overloaded
with clothes and it can barely move
in the tub of the machine or it gets all
out of whack by walking across the
floor pushing and shoving its way
around because it is off balance. You
look inside and the tub is all
cockeyed and tilted because of the
overload. Well that's the way we get
when we are off balance. God created
everything in balance: including the

earth, the moon and the stars and man too. When we get sick or in trouble, suddenly we are off balance. Let's move on.

When you 'dis' something, it is that you go against it; rebel or act out; a negative action. Dis-order opposed to order: and order is the opposite of disorder and we see that in the world today. They do not want to obey the rules or the laws of the land and that is branded as lawlessness in the Bible. There are four verses of scripture in the Book of Matthew alone:

1. Matthew 7:23

*And then I will declare to them, 'I never knew you; depart from Me, you who practice **lawlessness**!'*

2. Matthew 13:41

The Son of Man will send out His angels, and they will gather out of His kingdom all things that offend,

and those who
*practice **lawlessness**,*
3. Matthew 23:28

Even so you also outwardly appear
righteous to men, but inside you are
*full of hypocrisy and **lawlessness**.*

4. Matthew 24:12

*And because **lawlessness** will*
abound, the love of many will grow
cold.

This is disorder and sin. The root of
all of this including stress and
anxiety is fear based. Fear opens the
door to lawlessness! Do we not see
this today in our society in America?
They are afraid of everything and the
effects of this cause are lawlessness.
America must turn away and repent
of their sin although the Bible says
where sin abounds, grace abounds
more. We need much grace in
America!

Romans 5:20-21

20 Moreover the law entered that the offense might abound. But where sin abounded, grace abounded much more,

21 so that as sin reigned in death, even so grace might reign through righteousness to eternal life through Jesus Christ our Lord.

Let's pray:

Dear Jesus,
We grow close to You today,
As we repent of the disorder in our lives,
And ask you to help us,
Get back on track.
Heading straight towards you on that narrow path.
Thank You Lord that you will save America,
And restore our freedoms,
In Jesus mighty name,
Amen.

CHAPTER NINE

Stress is Not of God!

1 Corinthians 14:33
For God is not the author
of confusion but of peace, as in all
the churches of the saints.

What is stress? Many people experience this throughout their lives. I believe it is one of the opposites of peace and I don't want it if it is not of God. Stress sounds like another disorder, right? I know it is thrown around a lot in conversations. Let's define it here:

Stress
 noun

\ ˈstres \

Essential Meaning of *stress*

1: a state of mental tension and worry caused by problems in your life, work, etc. She uses meditation as a way of reducing/relieving *stress*. Hormones are released into the body in response to emotional *stress*. He needs help with *stress management*. [Ways to deal with stress]

2: something that causes strong feelings of worry or anxiety; I'm sorry for being grumpy. I've been *under* (a lot of) *stress* at work lately. She is dealing with the *stresses* of working full-time and going to school. He talked about the *stresses and strains* of owning a business.

3: physical force or pressure; Carrying a heavy backpack around all day puts a lot of *stress* on your shoulders and back. To reduce the amount of *stress* on your back, bend your knees when you lift something heavy. The ship's mast snapped *under the stress* of high winds; measuring the effects of *stresses* on the material

Stress is something you really need to refrain from because it too has varying effects on the body, mind and soul causing adverse sicknesses and disease to open up for you and in extreme cases can cause death. It is the opposite of peace that God gives us and Jesus died to give us. Stress, anxiety and fear are the opposing forces against the peace of God.

Peace will give you rest but these other disorders will cause chaos and turmoil in your life. I think about Jesus asleep in the stern of the boat as they crossed the tumultuous seas and the disciples were so afraid as the seas rose up higher and higher throwing the boat to and fro against the waves. The storm kept getting bigger as Jesus slept and was at peace. The disciples cried out to Jesus saying,

"Teacher, do You not care that we are perishing? (Mark 4:38)

Jesus got up and calmed the storm by saying, *"Peace, be still."* And the winds and seas calmed at the sound of His voice. (Mark 4:39)

Jesus answered, *"Why are you so fearful? How is it that you have no faith?"* (Mark 4-40)

Jesus does that same thing for us today by saying, *"O ye of little faith!"* We must have faith to take this journey today with Jesus and fear, stress or anxiety should never enter into the equation. Faith is the opposite of fear.

Trouble comes and we get stressed out and anxious. But the opposite must be, by seeking God first. The world has no answers to our troubles, but God waits for you to ask Him! Jesus has the solution to everything. He is our problem-solver if we but trust in Him!

Matthew 6:33
But seek first the kingdom of God
and His righteousness, and all these
things shall be added to you.

Stress is a type of overextension by overextending and upsetting our emotional balance. You remember that big rollercoaster you rode on bravely as a youngster; too young to know better? Now you've got your emotions involved riding up and down these wrong roads causing hypertension in your body and sickness to your mind. Come on now it is time to get it together and hand it all over to Jesus who will handle it so beautifully and with great care too. He cares so much for each one of us, and we must do it today!

1 Peter 5:7
Casting all your care upon him; for
he careth for you.

Jesus is the only way to get set free from all of these maladies. He says in John 14:6 He is the way, the truth and the life and no man comes to the

Father but by Him. I believe Him,
how about you? It's scriptural and it
is Jesus 100% and more. We must
stand together and fight these woes
as one Body. Remembering we are
the Body of Christ as He has knit us
together in His love.

Colossians 2:2
That their hearts might be
comforted, being knit together in
love, and unto all riches of the full
assurance of understanding, to the
acknowledgement of the mystery of
God, and of the Father, and of
Christ;

We are to follow Jesus!

Just in the Book of Matthew Jesus
speaks this 8 times. Throughout the
New Testament when Jesus walks
the earth, it is spoken of 39 times:
"Follow me!"

1. Matthew 4:19

And he saith unto them, **Follow me**, and I will make you fishers of men.

2. Matthew 8:22

But Jesus said unto him, **Follow me;** and let the dead bury their dead.

3. Matthew 9:9

And as Jesus passed forth from thence, he saw a man, named Matthew, sitting at the receipt of custom: and he saith unto him, **Follow me**. And he arose, and followed him.

4. Matthew 9:27

And when Jesus departed thence, two blind men **followed him,** crying, and saying, Thou son of David, have mercy on us.

5. Matthew 10:38

*And he that taketh not his cross, and **followeth after me**, is not worthy of me.*

6. Matthew 16:24

*Then said Jesus unto his disciples, If any man will come after me, let him deny himself, and take up his cross, and **follow me.***

7. Matthew 19:21

*Jesus said unto him, If thou wilt be perfect, go and sell that thou hast, and give to the poor, and thou shalt have treasure in heaven: and come and **follow me.***

8. Matthew 19:28

*And Jesus said unto them, Verily I say unto you, That ye which have **followed me**, in the regeneration when the Son of man shall sit in the throne of his glory, ye* *also shall sit upon twelve thrones, judging the twelve tribes of Israel.*

Somewhere along the line, we as God's people have forgotten who we are to follow? Can this be? Jesus is the One; He is the only One!

Let's pray...

Dear Jesus,
I know you are the way, the truth and the life,
And I need you to direct my steps.
I surrender all to you!
Dear Lord bring me to a place of submission,
So stress, anxiety or fear,
Will no longer live in my life!
Please close all doors to trauma,
And open up those marked,
Love, joy and peace for my sake.
Help me to follow You closer as the Bible says,
"Follow Me!"
In Jesus name, amen.

CHAPTER TEN

Rejoice, and Again I Say Rejoice!

Philippians 4:4-9
4 Rejoice in the Lord always: and again I say, Rejoice.

5 Let your moderation be known unto all men. The Lord is at hand.

6 Be careful for nothing; but in every thing by prayer and supplication with thanksgiving let your requests be made known unto God.

7 And the peace of God, which passeth all understanding, shall keep your hearts and minds through Christ Jesus.

8 Finally, brethren, whatsoever things are true, whatsoever things are honest, whatsoever things are just, whatsoever things are pure, whatsoever things are lovely, whatsoever things are of good report; if there be any virtue, and if there be any praise, think on these things.

9 Those things, which ye have both learned, and received, and heard, and seen in me, do: and the God of peace shall be with you.

There is nothing much better than to praise and worship the Lord; be happy in the Spirit and find joy along the way. *"Rejoice, and again I say rejoice!"* Sometimes we have to repeat ourselves to get ahead of the problematic days that are here. Joy in rejoicing can cause one to regain what the enemy has stolen. Don't allow him to rob you of your joy. It is your strength that he's going after;

for because we all know in *Nehemiah 8:10, "the joy of the Lord is our strength."* If the enemy of our soul robs us of our strength by taking our joy, we become defeated; downtrodden, depressed and destroyed! That is exactly what he wants! Why should we as believers in Christ play into the devil's hand of destruction? All glory to God, lift up holy hands and praise the Lord because He has given you life and life more abundant. (John 10:10) Don't forget the beautiful grace of God that has saved you for eternity.

  Get up out of the dumpster of life and raise your hands and praise Jesus because He is good! Lifting your hands is a sign of surrender unto our glorious God!

  God does not stutter but He repeats Himself in this scripture emphasizing to rejoice! There is so much power in praise and worship unto the Lord and a great reward in your heart to give it unto Him once more. These actions are reaping the benefits God has given us. To sit and mope around, feeling sorry for oneself is NOT one of these benefits. This is not good nor is it GOD! No one wants to come to a pity-party of one, do they? Step up, step out and rejoice because your joy will be restored and quickly too. Suddenly you will feel the Holy Spirit fill you again as you surrender in praise and worship and joy will come flooding back in.

Psalm 30:5
For his anger endureth but a moment; in his favour is life: weeping may endure for a night, but joy cometh in the morning.

It's morning time today and we all need to rejoice for the King will return for His Bride soon. Rejoicing is the opposite of all this book is about and I am so thankful we have alternatives to this gross darkness on the earth today. We have the great light of Jesus Christ, a light that will never go out and will always direct our steps.

Psalm 119:105
Thy word is a lamp unto my feet,
and a light unto my path.

Let's pray...

Dear Jesus,
Please receive our worship and praise unto YOU!
Help us to surrender, so we may reclaim what the enemy has stolen.
We want our joy back,
And the ability to step out of the enemies plan;
But instead allow us to submit to Your plan,
For our lives.
Thank You Lord for all the grace you have given us,
We will praise your holy name,
All of our days!
In Jesus mighty name amen!

CHAPTER ELEVEN

Everything That Can Be Shaken Will Be Shaken!

The world is in a test today as they have turned away from God! Thank God for the church that seeks God and prays. There is so much to do in this day and age of 2022; people are deluged by the sinful acts of others all around them as God protects them in His sacrosanct bubble, keeping the light on for all to see. Scripture alerts us to the fact that there will be a shaking and I have often heard preachers say, *"Everything that can be shaken, will be shaken!"* It's a tough spot to be in but the world today may need a good shaking to wake up from its sinfully rebellious life. Here are some scriptural references. I always turn to Psalms first because they are timeless:

Psalm 18:7
Then the earth shook and trembled;
The foundations of the hills also
quaked and were shaken, Because
He was angry.

AND

Matthew 24:29
The Coming of the Son of Man
"Immediately after the tribulation of those days the sun will be darkened, and the moon will not give its light; the stars will fall from heaven, and the powers of the heavens will be shaken."

AND

Mark 13:24-25
The Coming of the Son of Man
24 "But in those days, after that tribulation, the sun will be

*darkened, and the moon will not
give its light;*

*25 the stars of heaven will fall, and
the powers in the heavens will
be shaken.*

The Lord God of Heaven will do the
shaking and many will fall. Jesus will
return and evil will not come with
Him as He picks up His Bride to go
to The Marriage Supper of the Lamb.
Those who love the Lord will go with
Him. There will be no doubt or
hesitation.

*Revelation 19:9
Then he said to me, "Write:
'Blessed are those who are called to
the marriage supper of the Lamb!' "
And he said to me, "These are the
true sayings of God."*

I am writing this as scripture says,
*"Blessed are those who are called to
the marriage supper of the Lamb!"*

Let's get prepared for this supper
Heaven is preparing for us. Get

hungry and thirsty after God and negate the trials and the tribulations and give them over to the Lord. We have much to do yet; souls to win and wisdom to gain; forgiveness to give and joy to receive for the rest of our days here on earth. These tests shall strengthen us. In the Beatitudes which I love to quote in the Book of Matthew, chapter five, the sayings of Jesus gives us cause to be hungry:

Matthew 5:6
Blessed are they which
do hunger and thirst after
righteousness: for they shall be
filled.

Whatever will be shaken will not be necessary for us to survive, even flourish under the guide of our Lord and Savior. He said that He would never leave us nor forsake us and I for one believe Him because His sayings are true. What do you need shaken out of your life? Are there impurities in your Christian life of faith? Have you believed a lie that you know of or have you walked circumspectly around the lie to avoid its effects? Let's get right before the Lord today or He will shake that anxiety; fear and stress from you like a tornado wind coming through your town or city; shaking everything that must be shaken to fall away from this tree.

The Bible says confess your faults one to the other. It doesn't say to keep them top secret and hide them as long as you can, but reveal them in prayer to God. Confess to a praying friend! Give up that heavy load, don't hang onto it, but get rid of it! Let's glean from scripture in the Book of James:

James 5:14-16
14 Is any sick among you? let him call for the elders of the church; and let them pray over him, anointing him with oil in the name of the Lord:

15 And the prayer of faith shall save the sick, and the Lord shall raise him up; and if he have committed sins, they shall be forgiven him.

16 Confess your faults one to another, and pray one for another, that ye may be healed. The effectual fervent prayer of a righteous man availeth much.

Let's pray...

Dear Jesus,
We come in your mighty name,
We seek your wisdom,
And cast our cares upon you.
Father help save us during these tumultuous times,
And protect us from temptation and the evil one.
Thank you Lord for your angels camped around about us,
Thank you for our salvation and eternal life.
In Jesus name, amen.

CHAPTER TWELVE

The Door of Fear

There are some doors you had rather not open and fear is a gargantuan one that should NEVER be opened. Fear is the opposite of faith and if we are faith centered in our Creator then fear should never play a part of our lives which is easy to say and much harder to undo.

Fear is a tricky spirit that offers chaos and invites many other spirits to come in along with him. Spirits that cause tumult; sickness, disease, abuse, war and very generally tormenting those who allow this entrance.

JOB in the Bible is a good case of this although God said he was a fine man when satan approached God in Heaven about him. But satan cannot approach anyone about us if we have not opened some illegal door of entrée way. It is illegal for satan to come on our turf as believers because we have made Jesus our Lord and Savior unless we allow him in by anxiety, fear, stress or sin of any kind. This door was closed in salvation by Jesus but if you open these doors, any one of them then the attack becomes real. I often quote Job's life in scripture because of the extreme circumstances that were involved. Job said this in prayer:

Job 3:25
For the thing which I greatly feared is come upon me, and that which I was afraid of is come unto me.

Job acknowledged the fear in his life before God in prayer. He announced it out loud! Did God condemn him, oh no of course not.

We remember that He loves all of us especially those who serve Him and Job served God. But he, Job opened the door of fear and satan marched right in through that front door. Because Job announced his fear, this gave satan legal access to Job's life for he opened the door! Big mistake! He wreaked havoc in Job's life to the umpteenth degree and we cannot measure the pain and suffering that Job went through losing everything except his life. Good to keep your mouth shut!

Although God preserved his life and as miserable as it was, it took Job many conversations in scripture later, written for mankind's benefit to learn from this wise man's misfortunes. Who can commiserate with him? His latter was greater than his former, but the loss was inevitably soul drenching as he twisted and writhed in the pain of his body and his memories. It had to hurt although he never spoke against God as his wife did who spoke negatively saying, *"Why don't you curse God and die?"*

Job 2:9
Then said his wife unto him, Dost thou still retain thine integrity? curse God, and die.

Can you imagine this? Cursing God is a terrible enough thing to think on, much less to say. Job replies to his wife by calling her foolish. We don't ever hear what happened to her, but her words were piercing to Job as I am sure he expected her support and not her rebuke. Life goes on for Job as his friends come in to accuse him of all kinds of things but not once is fear mentioned or repented of: the door remains wide open.

Have you opened that big door of fear in your life and trouble has walked through to cause chaos in your life as you pray and continue to serve God? You who have opened this door needs deliverance because only God can do this and close this door permanently for you. A tormenting life is not the Christian's portion if and when they trust God. Do you trust God with your life?

Fear is a large stronghold in many lives today and we can see it by the hands of man who created this covid pandemic and left the door open to widespread fear. I was tempted yes I was; but I definitely knew whom I trusted and God led us through this time of great tumult in our world today. We are not of this world and it says this in scripture:

1 John 4:4
Ye are of God, little children, and have overcome them:
because greater is he that is in you, than he that is in the world.

Jesus proclaims in many scriptures that He is not of this world, but His Kingdom is of God. And so should we be. We cannot afford to entertain fear and all of its miserable companions and continue to live a good and fruitful life before God and man. We must kick it out! We must cast it out! Now how do we do that? We must speak it in Jesus mighty name and mean it and never take it back, ever. Ask Jesus to shut that door for eternity! He will do it! This is the kind of door you need opened, one direct to heaven:

Revelation 3:8
I know thy works: behold, I have set
before thee an open door,
and no man can shut it: for thou
hast a little strength, and hast kept
my word, and hast not denied my
name

Let God open the doors and you will be blessed; ask Him to close any man-made doors that are not of Him and keep you in His peace. He is the Lord of All and He will surely help you! Step out of fear and walk boldly into faith as His mercy and grace washes over you; you will find your way again.

2 Timothy 1:7
For God hath not given us
the spirit of fear; but of power,
and of love, and of a sound mind.

In the manner of fear, God has
given me something from the Bible
to pass along to you because of this
wide range of fear in this pandemic
state of covid and so many are afraid
to catch this virus. My husband and I
have both had it and although it was
a rough time, sickness of any kind is
never a pleasant picnic for anyone,
no matter who you are. We were
about one month getting completely
over it. It tried to become a cling-on
with us but we shook it off as soon as
we regained some of our strength. It
affected our whole church and our
fellowship time was shortened to
prevent more spreading of this
treacherous germ labeled covid-19.
They even gave it a number to
remember it by! Funny, this thing
really has no power against God!

There has recently been a
resurgence of this virus because the

first time around, had not caused enough deaths and it came around again a second time. Well our church as well as ourselves personally had enough antibodies to resist this second wave and very thankful we did. God is good, He equips us! We lost one friend from our church who died in the first round in the hospital from this virus, but his health was already in a compromised position. It was a terrible loss for all of us. His new wife is still in and out of hospitals suffering from these effects. Thankful he is with Jesus today, but his death still had an impact and deep sadness about it although we knew he was in a better place altogether.

Life goes on and the virus reared its ugly head again, losing friends and relatives that many knew and loved. Facebook was full of sympathetic postings due to the losses in so many different families. The church realm took a heavy blow as many pastors succumbed to this illness after going into the hospital because they lost their function to breathe in pneumonia and many breathing issues of the lungs and bronchial passages which filled up with this viral load and was deadly for so many. The churches are still reeling from these losses. People jumped right back into fear as they had the first time; shutting down churches, putting on masks and giving into this offensive virus which was the plague of our time and generation. So many are still quarantined, afraid to go out; getting vaccinated for further help and dying regardless, sad.

Some say the vaccinated stay in a viral flux giving off germs more than ever. There is a lot of supposition and theories on this plague we have suffered. We may never know the gist of all of this, this side of heaven because the real truth never comes out. Only God knows and He does speak through the prophets of our day and we need to listen and pay attention. And the church keeps praying; keeps believing for our Messiah to come and heal us once and for all. They are also hoping the rapture will be their final victory over this enemy.

I have a good friend who is very cautious not to go out because she has been sick with many other things which included cancer and any extraneous visits could compromise her healing if she caught covid; and after all of this, she is still operating in fear. This is far worse. If you open the door to fear, the virus can come strolling right in with your permission because after all you opened that door. Fear is a permission slip to the enemy; he can come right on it without any hindrance. For you opened the door yourself by your words and actions.

One question I would ask you right now is: *Didn't God give us a natural immunity system to fight off sickness and disease?"*

So what happened to it? What was the compromise we as mankind did to change God's system? SIN! This is the answer to all our troubles. We need to lay it all down and take up the cross.

The Lord has given me some scriptures that brought reality to my spirit as those who fear and tremble over covid are in serious trouble. I don't mean those who are cautious, but I mean those who truly fear. Let's set this up by looking to Jesus as the Lord who led me by His Spirit to those leprous scriptures in the New Testament, now I will relate them to you: In the Book of Matthew there are four different scriptures to study:

Jesus Cleanses the Leper
Matthew 8:1-2

1 When He had come down from the mountain, great multitudes followed Him.

2 And behold, a leper came and worshiped Him, saying, "Lord, if You are willing, You can make me clean."

Matthew 10:8
Heal the sick, cleanse the lepers,
raise the dead, cast out demons.
Freely you have received, freely
give.

AND
Matthew 11:5
The blind see and the lame
walk; the lepers are cleansed
and the deaf hear; the dead are
raised up and the poor have the
gospel preached to them

AND

Matthew 26:6-7
The Anointing at Bethany

6 And when Jesus was in Bethany at
the house of Simon the leper,

7 a woman came to Him having an
alabaster flask of very costly
fragrant oil, and she poured it on
His head as He sat at the table.

And in the Book of Luke:

Luke 17:11-12
Ten Lepers Cleansed

11 Now it happened as He went to Jerusalem that He passed through the midst of Samaria and Galilee. 12 Then as He entered a certain village, there met Him ten men who were lepers, who stood afar off.

Jesus walked with lepers, cleansed and healed them. He never ran from them; turned from them or put on a mask to treat them and make them whole again! Who are we following again?

Jesus sat at the table of Simon the leper preparing to eat with him. He was later anointed by the Woman with the Alabaster Box at meet. She poured her costly substance of oil upon Him at this table. This was oil valued at approximately one year's wages in those days. She readied Him for burial they say, because soon He was going to the cross of crucifixion and give His life.

In the Book of Luke Jesus healed the ten lepers as He walked to Jerusalem. Jesus was not afraid of their contagious nature. Are we not followers of Jesus? Are we not to do greater things? How can we if we walk in fear? We must really readjust our measure of faith if we are to walk in the power that Jesus walked in. Neither sickness nor disease ever touched Him.

1 Corinthians 6:19
Or do you not know that your body is the temple of the Holy Spirit who is in you, whom you have from God, and you are not your own?

LEPROSY VS COVID

How is it so different, both kill? Jesus defeats both on the cross of Calvary. His life for ours was sacrificed. Do not deny the cross by standing in fear today. Our lives are hidden in Christ! Get up and get out!

Let's pray...

Dear Jesus,
We come in your holy name,
Walk us out through the door of
fear,
And slam it shut for us!
We want no part of it,
But want the fulness of the Spirit,
You have given us.
Forgive us for doubting,
And keep us in your love and grace.
In Jesus mighty name,
Amen.

CHAPTER THIRTEEN

Pray About Everything!

Pray without ceasing the Bible says and that seems nearly impossible in this busy world today. But if you are in constant contact with the Lord then there is communication coming and going from Heaven to Earth; from you to Him from Him to you. This is prayer. This is seeking *Abba's* advice and wisdom, yes it is. Life is so much better when we stay connected to the heart of God and His influence is in and around us and we will never circumvent His system of good. We stay rooted and grounded in the Word of God! We build our house upon the Rock, steady and sure.

Matthew 26:41
Watch and pray, that ye enter not into temptation: the spirit indeed is willing, but the flesh is weak.

There is nothing that you cannot give God because He already knows your thoughts, and your needs. We have established in earlier chapters that He searches your heart, so He knows your heart so, so well. Draw close to Him and pray! We wrote a book some time ago in 2019:

"It's Never Too Late To Pray!"

We are reminded of Lazarus, because he was dead, buried in a tomb and stunk those 4 days and by the time Jesus raised him from the dead before his sisters Mary and Martha, God was glorified. Prayers can cause miracles if spoken in Jesus mighty name. There is nothing good God will withhold from you.

Lazarus got sick and Jesus waited four days before He came to revive him, a good friend. I know with God there is always a plan and a purpose in all He does. God the Father did not allow Jesus to go forth quickly, during the sickness of Lazarus. It was certainly so because He could raise Him and raise the faith of others so they might do the same today. It was a miracle of miracles for all mankind to see! For me it takes a lot of faith to raise the dead, this precious miracle of breathing back life into a lifeless body was way beyond the norm. This was a bit of a frightening endeavor I would think for most to observe, read about, and much less perform.

Today many are dying from the man-made plague of covid cooked up in some laboratory on foreign soil, to kill the weak and fearful as they succumb to the malice of it all. God sets before us life and death in scripture and I feel many times, it could be our choices that hinder us;

our fear that actually kills us before our time:

Deuteronomy 30:19-20
19 I call heaven and earth to record this day against you, that I have set before you life and death, blessing and cursing: therefore choose life, that both thou and thy seed may live:

20 That thou mayest love the LORD thy God, and that thou mayest obey his voice, and that thou mayest cleave unto him: for he is thy life, and the length of thy days: that thou mayest dwell in the land which the LORD sware unto thy fathers, to Abraham, to Isaac, and to Jacob, to give them

CHOOSE LIFE!

This life we have is God-given as He created us; He chose us, knew us and as He breathed life into us; so God's wisdom says choose life today. This book addresses many issues that we have been facing on a daily basis, but we must know whom we serve. We must have a keen relationship with Father; given through Jesus Christ the Son and empowered by the Holy Spirit and firepower. We have been given something so super special that this life here on earth is but 'a vapor' the Bible calls it until we go to be with Jesus in eternity. We will live forever.

Our bodies were not built for forever here on earth, but our spirits were and we will live with Jesus forever as He does today, seated at the right-hand of the Father making intercession for the saints. We must employ prayer. It is a must do! How else may we live? Prayer is our life-line to heaven for the best life God has to offer minus fear, anxiety, strife, stress and anger; for the cares of the world belong to God as we cast them unto Him. He takes them gladly.

Prayer is that concept, as I can recall early on in my walk with Jesus, one of the first things I wanted to learn to do, was to pray. God sent me people in my life who taught me, who supported me and my efforts to pray. It became better and better until today when I enjoy praying with Father so much.

"It's Never Too Late To Pray!" Book excerpt:

"God has given us the heart to pray. This is how we learn to communicate with Him. There is never a time that is not good to pray. You can turn around and pray again, your Father is always waiting to hear from you, again and again. Prayer is for everyone and we felt the urgency to write these things that have helped my husband and I on our walk with Jesus. We wanted to produce a simple hand book for many who needed help to pray. To communicate with our Father, the Son and with the Holy Spirit who helps us and teaches us. We hope this helps you."

Jesus promises us in the Word of God that we will do greater things than He. Can you imagine this? That is why it is never too late to pray because your faith can move mountains; cure cancer; change hearts and minds; cast out devil spirits and send peace back into the spirit of another person. What benefit is it to keep quiet when you could say a prayer to save someone from the pit of hell or a lifetime of torment. Your prayer may cause God's hand to move on behalf of that person who has the need.

John 1:50
Jesus answered and said to him, "Because I said to you, 'I saw you under the fig tree,' do you believe? You will see greater things than these."

There will always be greater things to come but no one will ever come greater than Jesus; He is the King of Kings and the Lord of Lords and there is none like Him. Lift His name up in prayer today as you give everything over to Him, your cares will evaporate and you will be filled with His Spirit free and clear.

If you have a need today or know others who do, lift up a heart-felt prayer towards heaven asking in the name of Jesus, until its answered and answered fully according to God's will and not man's. Persevere towards the answer needed.

Let's pray...

Dear Jesus,
We come in your lovely name,
And we pray to you.
Know our hearts and please
Answer our prayers.
We give you all:
Anxiety, fear and stress we may have,
And leave it with you for good!
We will not pick it back up,
Jesus clean up our lives for good.
In Jesus name, amen.

Colossians 2:6-7
6 As you therefore have
received Christ Jesus the Lord,
so walk in Him,

7 rooted and built up in Him
and established in the faith, as
you have been taught,
abounding in it with
thanksgiving.

PRAYER of SALVATION

Let's pray together...

Lord Jesus, I confess that I am a sinner and in need of salvation. I believe that You came to earth to seek and to save people who are lost in their sins, and I believe that You died on the cross as the substitute for my sins.

I believe that You took the punishment that I deserved for the sins that I have committed, and forgave me all my sins. I believe that You died for me and that You rose again from the dead, and that whoever believes in You will not perish but have everlasting life.

I trust in You and I place my faith in You. Thank You for dying for me, forgiving my sins, making me clean and covering me in Your own perfect righteousness. Thank You for all that You have done for me.

I receive You into my life as my Saviour and I choose to follow You and serve You all my life. Thank You for hearing my prayer,

Amen.

AUTHOR'S CORNER

Susan J Perry born January 12, 1952 in Niskayuna, New York and resided in Schenectady, NY most of her early life. She graduated from Schalmont High School in Rotterdam, NY in 1970. She was saved to Jesus in the fall of 1998 in Houston, Texas where she lived for twenty-five years. She now lives for Jesus in Edgewater, Florida for fifteen years, writing as she is inspired to do so. She is married to Pastor John R Perry. In their blended marriage they have four children and five grandchildren scattered all over the United States, healthy, happy and doing well.

She serves Bishop William T. White as her Pastor in The Edgewater Church of God, as well as her husband. This church loves Jesus and His people and while on assignment there, she has written many books. Now she and her husband publish their books as well as others books in: **Simply This Publishing.** They publish the good news of Jesus Christ in book form while in hardcover, paperback and Kindle version, they live the life as well.

Isaiah 61:1-3
The Good News of Salvation

1 "The Spirit of the Lord GOD is upon Me, Because the LORD has anointed Me To preach good tidings to the poor; He has sent Me to heal the

brokenhearted, To proclaim liberty
to the captives, And the opening of
the prison to those who are bound;

2 To proclaim the acceptable year of
the LORD,
And the day of vengeance of
our God;
To comfort all who mourn,

3 To console those who mourn
in Zion,
To give them beauty for ashes,
The oil of joy for mourning,
The garment of praise for the spirit
of heaviness;
That they may be called trees of
righteousness,
The planting of the LORD, that He
may be glorified."

Their pulpit is behind the computer
tapping the keys, creating books to
help others. God gives them so many
benefits to share in the Body of
Christ. John and Susan both teach at
their church and occasionally at
other churches; woman's meetings
and whenever asked, they go.

CONTACT THE PERRY'S

1 Corinthians 14:3
But he who prophesies speaks
edification and exhortation and
comfort to men

All available on www.Amazon.com
Kindle Direct Publishing
Simply This Publishing
John & Susan Perry
Edgewater, Florida

Contact info:

Susan J Perry, Email:
susiebqt987p@yahoo.com
& Facebook; Simply This Publishing

John R Perry, Email:
jperry8@bellsouth.net

ALL BOOKS AVAILABLE ON AMAZON.COM

Books can also be ordered through
bookstores and big box stores if that

is your preference. There is always a way.

In Florida our books are available in:

From My Library 2 URS

3510 S Nova Road, Suite # 107

Port Orange, Florida 32129

Proprietors: Samuel & Susan Titera

PERRY'S BOOKSHELF

The Samaritan Woman Testifies
Kindle only: $9.95

Simply This: The World's Greatest Message
Paperback: $5.95 Kindle: $3.99

Preach It Sister Girl!
Paperback: $9.95 Kindle: $5.99

ASK for WISDOM: The Safe Harbor of God
Paperback: $9.95 Kindle: $5.99

A Stone's Throw Away: A Woman Testifies
Paperback: $12.95 Kindle: $6.99

The Persistent Widow Testifies
Paperback: $12.95 Kindle: $6.99

The Woman Presenting the Alabaster Box Testifies
Paperback: $12.95 Kindle: $6.99

Great Holes in Your Pockets: Recovering All!
Paperback: $9.95 Kindle $5.99

Hidden in the Cleft of the Rock: A Woman Testifies
Paperback: $12.95 Kindle: $6.99

Daughters of Inheritance Testify
Paperback: $12.95 Kindle: $6.99

This Project is Called: HONOR
Paperback: $9.95 Kindle: $5.99

Our Experiences With ANGELS
Paperback $9.95 Kindle $5.99

The Double-Dip Blessings
Paperback $9.95 Kindle $5.99

It's Never Too Late To Pray
Paperback $5.95 Kindle $2.99

I AM A DUCK!
Paperback $9.95 Kindle $5.95

The Woman Touching the Hem of His Garment Testifies
Paperback $12.95 Kindle $6.99

This is the Anemic Church
Paperback $9.95 Kindle $5.99

There is a Witness!
Paperback $9.95 Kindle $5.99

Heal Them ALL! The Children's Portion
Paperback $7.95 Kindle $3.99

Ye Shall Serve God Upon This Mountain!
Paperback $9.95 Kindle $5.99

Thanksgiving Is Best!
Paperback $7.95 Kindle $3.99

The ABC'S of Perry
Paperback for kids $12.95

LOVE is Surely the Way
Paperback $7.95 Kindle $3.99

Lessons In Deliverance
Paperback $12.95 Kindle $6.99

Cancel Cancer: And The Effects Thereof
Paperback $9.95 Kindle $5.99

Royalty BELONGS To The Believer!
Paperback $9.95 Kindle $5.99

"Just When Did This Happen?"
Paperback $9.95 Kindle $5.99

I Declare Over You in Jesus Name
Paperback $5.95 Kindle $3.99

With Blessing & Favour Will You Compass Me About!
Paperback $9.95 Kindle $5.99

Going Down The Barker Road Missing...
Paperback $9.95 Kindle $5.99

Deception of Man: Sin Lies At The Door

Hard cover $15.95 Paperback $12.95 Kindle $6.99

Beautiful Things: Out Of The Dust

Paperback $9.95 Kindle $5.99

In My Weakness God is Strong:
Declarations of Strength: 60 Days

Paperback $15.95 Kindle $8.99

The Year of 2022: A Miraculous Work!
60 Day Devotional

Hardcover $15.95 Paperback $12.95 Kindle $6.99

Love Endures Devotional:
60 Day Devotional

Paperback $12.95 Kindle $6.99

Baking A Cake With God's Ingredients

Hardcover $15.95 Paperback $12.95 Kindle $8.99

TRAUMA: The Doors Opened to a Unique Spirit
Hardcover $15.95 Paperback $12.95 Kindle $6.99

The Holy Spirit Is Our Comforter
Paperback $12.95 Kindle $6.99

Be Anxious For Nothing: But Pray About Everything!
Paperback $9.95 Kindle $5.99